OK BOOMER

A SURVIVAL GUIDE FOR THE
MISUNDERSTOOD MILLENNIAL

summersdale

OK BOOMER

An Hachette UK Company
www.hachette.co.uk

Summersdale Publishers Ltd
Part of Octopus Publishing Group Limited
Carmelite House
50 Victoria Embankment
LONDON
EC4Y 0DZ
UK

www.summersdale.com

Printed and bound in the Czech Republic

ISBN: 978-1-78783-615-0

INTRODUCTION

Let's face it: no one generation will ever fully understand another. But when baby boomers suddenly start mocking millennials and our ways, something must be done!

Cue: "OK boomer" – the one and only phrase you'll ever need for when you JUST CAN'T with boomers any more.

With tips on spotting a boomer, definitions of their most out-of-touch phrases, and advice on the most suitable times to clap back with "OK boomer", this guide will ensure you're always prepared when hit with their bothersome jibes.

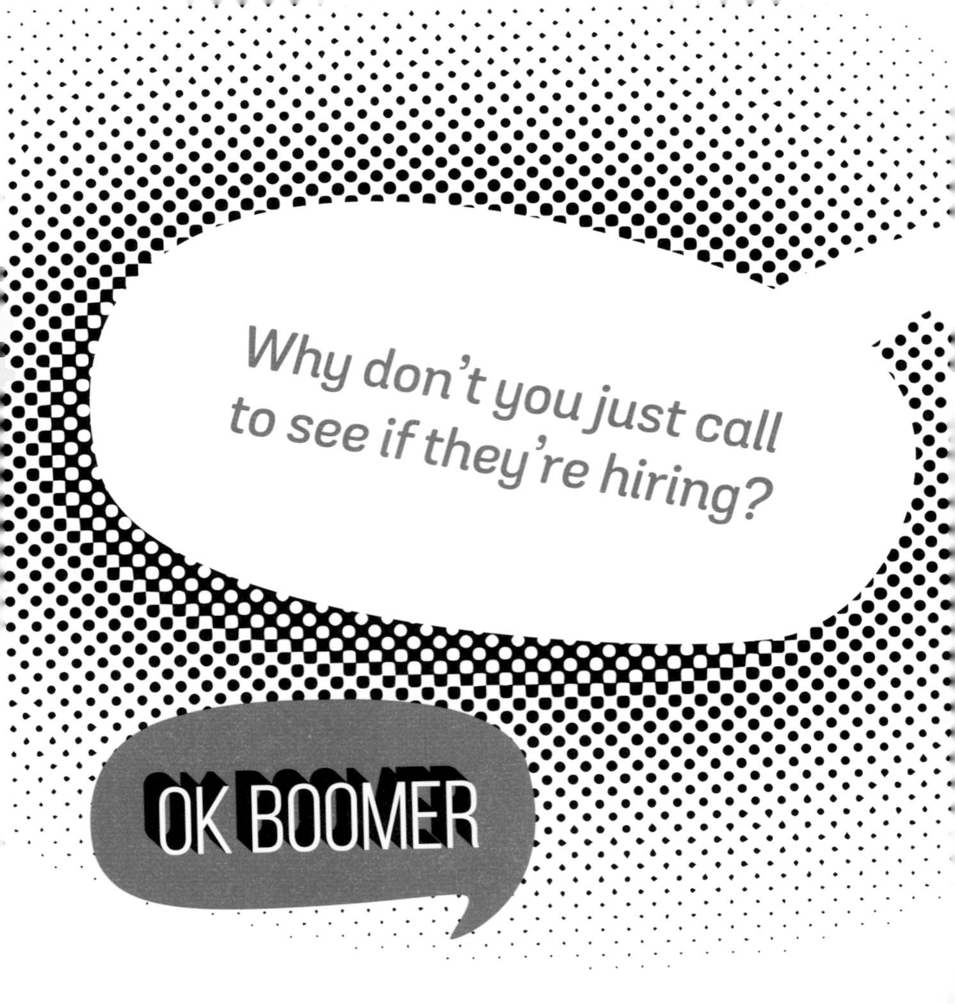
Why don't you just call to see if they're hiring?
OK BOOMER

HOW TO IDENTIFY A BOOMER:

A PHONE CASE THAT OPENS UP LIKE A BOOK

I suspect this
veganism malarkey
is just another fad.

OK BOOMER

A term used by baby boomers to imply that you are being oversensitive because you take offence to things that are, quite often, a bit offensive. Teacher patronizing you in front of everyone, making you feel embarrassed and self-conscious? Snowflake. Can't eat your lunch because the bread isn't gluten-free and you're at risk of having an allergic reaction? Snowflake. Don't want to attend that party because social situations make you anxious? Snowflake! Damn you and your compassion!

I thought that going to university would get you a proper job?

OK BOOMER

HOW TO IDENTIFY A BOOMER:

USES THEIR TABLET TO TAKE PHOTOS ON A TRIP

You'd have enough to get on the property ladder if you didn't waste so much money on avocados, sushi and coffee.

OK BOOMER

Savings? What's the meaning of this strange word, I hear you ask? The assumption of the boomer is that you've been able to set aside a minimum of 70 per cent of your monthly earnings and now have a large sum of money to dip into when you need it. Not the case? That's probably because you've been spending all your money on avocado toast and cocktails that glow in the dark – or just plain living.

Why don't you choose a job that's a bit closer to home?

OK BOOMER

HOW TO IDENTIFY A BOOMER:

A TAN **ALL YEAR ROUND**

Tinder? In my day, we had to ask someone out face-to-face.

OK BOOMER

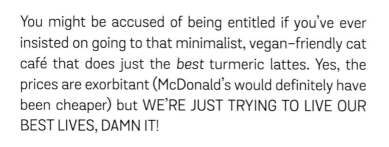

You might be accused of being entitled if you've ever insisted on going to that minimalist, vegan-friendly cat café that does just the *best* turmeric lattes. Yes, the prices are exorbitant (McDonald's would definitely have been cheaper) but WE'RE JUST TRYING TO LIVE OUR BEST LIVES, DAMN IT!

I could do with some global warming, thank you very much. It's too cold outside, if you ask me.

OK BOOMER

HOW TO IDENTIFY A BOOMER:

WHITE, KNEE-LENGTH SHORTS (COMPLETE WITH VPL)

Shared housing? At your age? That's just silly talk.

OK BOOMER

This will often be used in the same breath as "snowflake" and has become a phrase that can apply to pretty much any negative experience. For example, it's often heard at the returns counter, when the sales assistant isn't able to issue a refund on a well-worn cardigan due to store policy. Or you might even hear it in a restaurant, when the boomer's desired meal only comes as a vegan option.

If childcare is so expensive, why doesn't one of you give up work to stay at home and look after the kids?

OK BOOMER

HOW TO IDENTIFY A BOOMER:

HAS AN
IMMACULATE LAWN

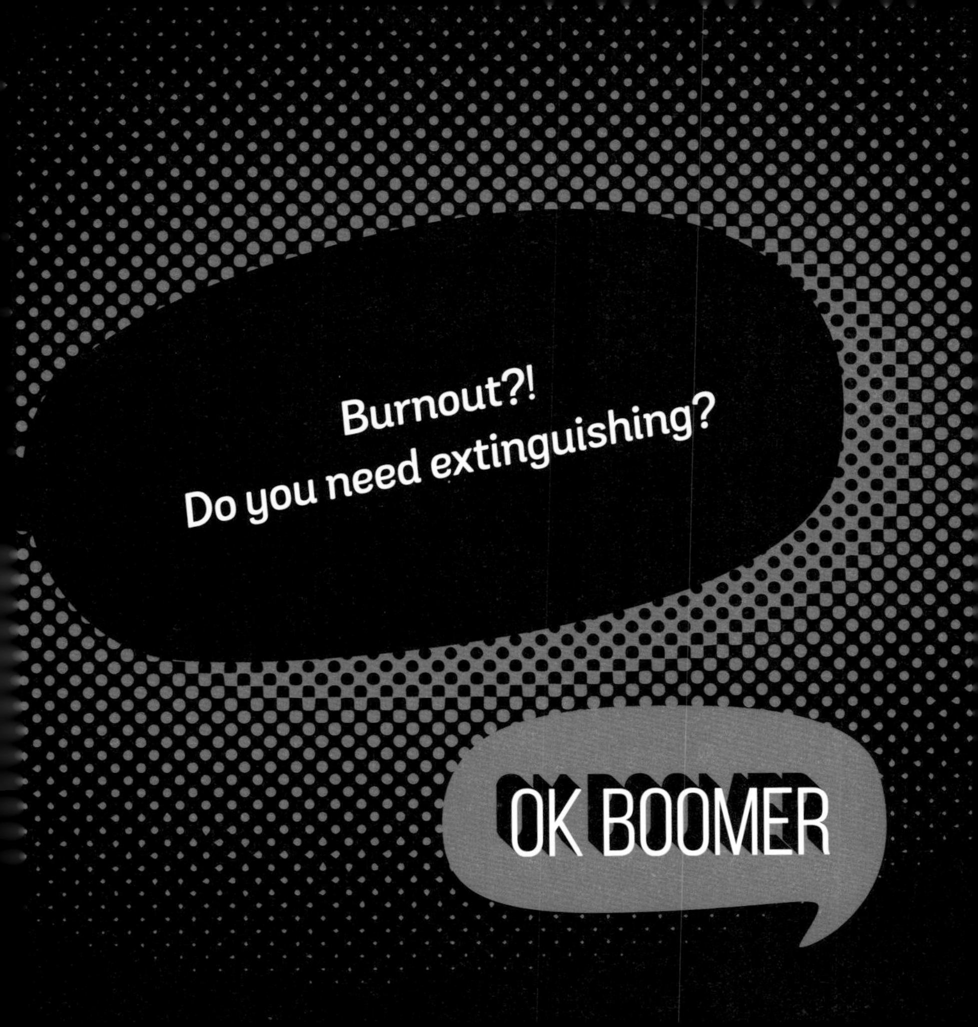
Burnout?!
Do you need extinguishing?
OK BOOMER

Often preceded by a *tut*, this phrase may be used in a number of scenarios – in response to you using your phone as a calculator instead of dividing a bill by 15 in your head, or using Google Maps instead of a giant printed one – but it is most commonly deployed when the boomer realizes that you don't recognize some outdated technology or equipment from their younger days. For instance, "I bet you don't remember what a floppy disk is... That's sad." Don't be downhearted – they're just embarrassed that they didn't know what kombucha is!

Netflix? In my day TV had three channels and they were all in black and white.

OK BOOMER

HOW TO IDENTIFY A BOOMER:

A SLEEVELESS JACKET
(LIKELY REFERRED TO AS
A "GILET" BUT PROBABLY
MISPRONOUNCED)

Kids these days are addicted to their phones – you should get some exercise instead.

OK BOOMER

If you're in your twenties and enjoy looking at memes instead of pulling your hair out over how you're ever going to afford this month's phone bill (racked up so high from looking at said memes), the boomer will almost certainly accuse you of having Peter Pan syndrome. You're an adult, for crying out loud! Don't you think it's time to leave the video games behind and jump on that property ladder?

You need a few minutes to "decompress"? For goodness' sake, you're not a gas!

OK BOOMER

HOW TO IDENTIFY A BOOMER:

**CRUISES AROUND
WITH THE TOP DOWN
ON ANY GIVEN MILDLY
WARM DAY**

Surely you've set aside enough for your pension by now?

OK BOOMER

MILLENNIALS HAVE KILLED...

Ah yes, that familiar refrain. Anything can be inserted to complete it — department stores, bar soap, exorcisms — because boomers believe that millennials are starving every industry out of existence, deliberately! How dare we spend money on rent and food instead of diamonds, golf and extravagant weddings?! Soon there will be nothing that the millennial hasn't laid their deadly hands on (except for houseplants — millennials love a good houseplant).

You're in your mid-twenties and I still don't have any grandchildren?!

OK BOOMER

HOW TO IDENTIFY A BOOMER:

THE CLASSIC
BEIGE CARDIGAN

I'll play you some
real music – none of
that electronic noise!

OK BOOMER

This usually means something along the lines of: "Your argument is *probably* valid, but it doesn't sound very nice, does it?! All this negativity – I'll just shut the conversation down now."

Never mind the hole in the ozone layer – let me sew up those holes in your jeans.

OK BOOMER

HOW TO IDENTIFY A BOOMER:

USUALLY FOUND ON A GOLF COURSE (COMPLETE WITH CLUB MEMBERSHIP)

The problem with young people today is that they have it too easy.

OK BOOMER

THE GOOD
OLD DAYS

Ahh, the good old days — that time when everything was significantly *better*. The baby boomer will often use this term when your newfangled technology fails you, or you've gone months communicating with friends without even seeing them face-to-face. The joke's on them, though, because we've grown up with Netflix.

Oh, sweetheart, still single? You should get out more.
OK BOOMER

HOW TO IDENTIFY A BOOMER:

SOCKS WITH SANDALS

I'm sure you'll be able to afford it — shall I put you in touch with my financial adviser?

OK BOOMER

PUT SOME ELBOW
GREASE INTO IT

Didn't you know? The answer to all your problems is elbow grease! If you simply put some effort into it, you'd be sure to find that high-flying executive position or the funds to buy a brand-new hatchback. It's got nothing to do with the economy at all! Really, it's the only factor stopping you from realizing your goals.

Three rounds of interviews?!
No, you don't want to work
somewhere like that.

OK BOOMER

HOW TO IDENTIFY A BOOMER:

TEXTS USING ONLY THEIR INDEX FINGER

All you have to do is work hard and you'll be set for life.

OK BOOMER

By saying this, the boomer is suggesting that you're being too sensitive and must therefore have no sense of humour. We're not quite sure where the boomer got this idea from, though. After all, millennials invented the meme, the funniest thing that's ever happened to the internet. And don't even get us started on GIFs!

You wouldn't catch me living at home at your age. I moved out at 18 because I wanted my independence!

OK BOOMER

IMAGE CREDITS

If you're interested in finding out more about our books, find us on Facebook at **Summersdale Publishers** and follow us on Twitter at **@Summersdale**.

www.summersdale.com